The Fisherman's Wife

Don't be greedy!

by Alison Hedger

Moral: Being greedy won't make you happy
Adapted from the traditional Brothers Grimm tale
A mixture of song, chanting in rap style, choral speaking, improvised
percussion, mime and narration
For School Assemblies and End of Term Entertainments
KS1 and Lower KS2
Approximately 10 minutes
The songs are sung by everyone
This book includes the words and music, a CD containing the story, demonstration versions and backing tracks for all the songs, a game and a craft idea.
Lyrics and script can be downloaded free of charge from our website at
www.goldenapplemusic.com/bitesize

THE MUSIC

Published by
Golden Apple Productions
8/9 Frith Street, London W1D 3JB, England.

Exclusive Distributors:
Music Sales Limited
Distribution Centre, Newmarket Road, Bury St Edmunds, Suffolk IP33 3YB, England.
Music Sales Corporation
257 Park Avenue South, New York, NY10010, United States of America.
Music Sales Pty Limited
120 Rothschild Avenue, Rosebery, NSW 2018, Australia.

Order No. GA11572
ISBN 1-84449-459-4
This book © Copyright 2004 by Golden Apple Productions.

Cover design by Butterworth Design
Music processed by Camden Music
Printed in the United Kingdom

Cast

Narrator(s)
Fisherman
Fisherman's Wife   speaking
Fish   speaking
Ladies from the dress shop
Bankers
Estate Agents
Musicians   with a selection of school percussion instruments
                                        4 groups: sun, rain, wind and storm

Props

- Fishing nets and a broom
- Selection of brightly coloured clothing with one especially outrageous dress for the Fisherman's wife to quickly put on
- Trays and bags of money and gold bullion bars in a barrow
- Estate Agent's particulars of very large properties

Costumes

These need not be elaborate, especially if you are performing this musical as part of a school assembly. One piece of costume should be sufficient to denote the various characters (hats, scarves, bow ties *etc.*)

- The fish will need a cardboard cut-out as tall as the child playing the part. A circle is cut out for the child's face

N.B. Minimal directions are given – the mime, entrances and exits follow the story.

Opening Link Music

with no added school percussion

This music acts as a link between the different episodes of the story, and subsequently has added percussion from the musicians to reflect the differing weather conditions as indicated in the script.

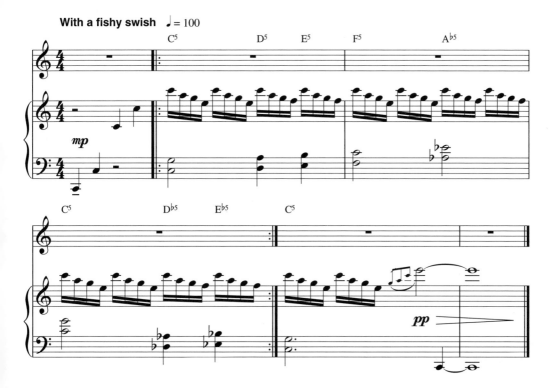

All the cast stand.

The Fisherman and his wife are to the front acting out some everyday chores, such as sweeping the floor, mending nets etc. The Fisherman's wife looks fed up and distinctly disgruntled.

Give Me More, More, More

real-ly nice guy.＿ She was greed-y, a fright - ful pain. You'd

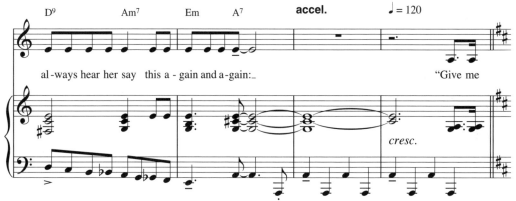

Optional Glockenspiel ends

accel. ♩ = 120

al -ways hear her say this a - gain and a-gain:＿ "Give me

cresc.

more, more, more, I'm fed up as I am. I wish I was mar - ried to a

5

ver - y wealth - y man. Give me more, more, more, I'm fed up as I am. I

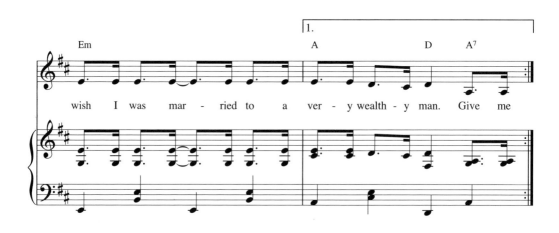

1.

wish I was mar - ried to a ver - y wealth - y man. Give me

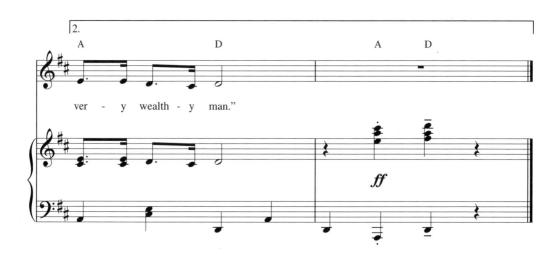

2.

ver - y wealth - y man."

_ff_

Link Music

with light and "sunny" added percussion

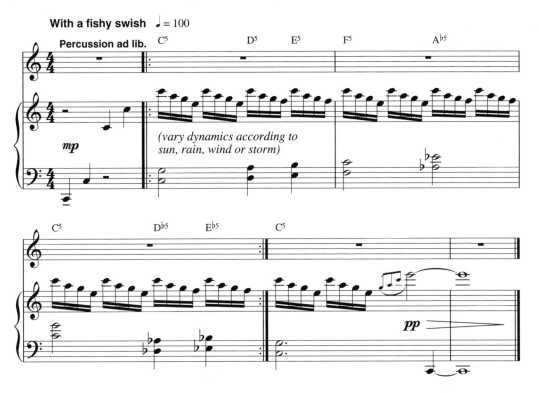

NARRATOR: One *sunny* afternoon an enormous fish was caught.
The Fisherman was stunned as the fish began to talk.

FISH: I'm a special magic fish,
With a special fishy wish.
Make a single wish today,
And I'll grant it right away.

ALL: A talking fish, how can this be?
No good will come – just wait and see.

NARRATOR: The Fisherman dropped the huge fish back into the sea and ran
to tell his wife that they had a special fishy wish! The
Fisherman's wife didn't hesitate. Without bothering to ask her
husband, she wished straight away for some beautiful, stunning
and very expensive clothes.

FISHERMAN'S WIFE: I want some fancy clothes – now!

Enter the Ladies from the dress shop with a large variety of frocks, skirts, blouses, hats etc...

Song

Frills And Flounces

At a very steady pace ♩. = 65

Frills and floun-ces, skirts that do boun-ces; cot - ton, sat - in, shim-mer-ing silk. All these clothes are yours for the tak - ing. We ev - en have a tar - tan kilt. Won-der-ful clothes you'll wear for ev - er. Be - lieve this lie, and you're_ not clev-er!

The Fisherman's wife quickly puts on the outrageously extravagant dress.

Link Music
with "rainy" sounds from the percussion

NARRATOR: One *rainy* afternoon an enormous fish was caught.
The Fisherman was stunned as the fish began to talk.

FISH: I'm a special magic fish,
With a special fishy wish.
Make a single wish today,
And I'll grant it right away.

ALL: A talking fish, how can this be?
No good will come – just wait and see.

NARRATOR: The Fisherman dropped the huge fish back into the sea and ran
to tell his wife the good news. They had another fishy wish. The
Fisherman's wife didn't hesitate. Without bothering to ask her
husband, she wished straight away for piles of money.

FISHERMAN'S WIFE: I want money – now!

Enter the Bankers with their trays, bags and barrow of money and gold bars.

Song Bags Of Money

At a very steady pace ♩. = 65

Bags of mon - ey, gold bars in bar - rows, sil - ver, dia - monds piled in a heap. You will nev - er be short of a pen - ny. Come and en - joy, it's yours_ to keep. Won - der - ful mon - ey will last for ev - er. Be - lieve this lie, and you're_ not clev - er!

Bankers exit leaving the money in a large heap.

Link Music
with "windy" sounds from the percussion

NARRATOR: One *windy* afternoon an enormous fish was caught.
The Fisherman was stunned as the fish began to talk.

FISH: I'm a special magic fish,
With a special fishy wish.
Make a single wish today,
And I'll grant it right away.

ALL: A talking fish, how can this be?
No good will come – just wait and see.

NARRATOR: The Fisherman dropped the huge fish back into the sea and ran
to tell his wife the good news. They had another fishy wish. The
Fisherman's wife didn't hesitate. Without bothering to ask her
husband, she wished straight away for the biggest, most
expensive house available.

FISHERMAN'S WIFE: I want a big house – now!

Enter Estate Agents with their particulars.

Song

This Big House

Exit Estate Agents.

Link Music

with "stormy" sounds from the percussion

NARRATOR: One *stormy* afternoon an enormous fish was caught.
The Fisherman was stunned as the fish began to talk.

FISH: I'm a special magic fish,
With a special fishy wish.
Make a single wish today,
And I'll grant it right away.

ALL: A talking fish, how can this be?
No good will come – just wait and see.

NARRATOR: The Fisherman dropped the huge fish back into the sea and ran
to tell his wife the good news. They had yet another fishy wish.
The Fisherman's wife didn't hesitate. Without bothering to ask
her husband, she wished straight away that she was Queen of
the whole world.

FISHERMAN'S WIFE: I want to be the Queen – now!

Everyone gasps in horror and amazement.

NARRATOR: Well, even the Fish was horrified by this last greedy wish.

Enter Fish with look of horror on his face.

Hadn't the Fisherman's wife had lots of fine clothes, more gold
than anyone else and a huge mansion to live in? To ask to be
the Queen of the whole world was just too much! So the Fish
stood still and thought hard… then he said….

FISH: "NO"

NARRATOR: She can't be Queen of the whole world, but she can be Queen of
her life as it used to be. In an instant everything was just as it
was before.

The fancy dress is taken away and the pile of money is removed.

The Fisherman and his wife were poor once again, but now they
were happy. Do you know what? The Fisherman's wife saw
riches in simple things and she became happy and unselfish.
She became the Queen of her simple life.

Big smiles from the Fisherman's wife.

Song **Don't Be Greedy**

With a heavy beat ♩ = 120

Don't be greed - y, greed - y's not nice.__ It makes you self - ish, so stop and think twice__ be - fore you say "I want, I__ wish",__ re - mem - ber that clev - er mag - i - cal fish.__ He

Lyrics under the music:
taught this les - son, nev - er just moan__ a - bout the things you'd
like to__ own.__ Be like that fish - er - wife who re - al - ised__ that
poor but hap - py, is twice as__ wise.__

(Older children will enjoy playing this melody on recorders.)

ALL CAST: Don't be greedy!
(smiling and waving)

THE END

GAME
Flapping Fish

Cut out fish shapes from tissue paper (or newspaper if preferred). The children form into two teams standing in a queue, with a long empty floor space to the front. Each child has a fish paper shape. On the start signal (a whistle), the first child from each team places their fish behind the starting line (piece of string) and with a "flapper" made from rolled up newspaper, creates a draught to flap their fish along, down the room to the finishing line (another piece of string). Once their fish is safely over the finish they run back and hand the "flapper" to the second child in their team, who flaps their own fish down the room to the finishing line. The winning team is the first to get all their fish over the finish line. No cheating is allowed – this game can get very noisy if the children cheer their team on!

CRAFT
Pretty Scaly Fish

• Coloured Paper
• Glue Stick
• Cardboard fish shapes

Cut lots of small squares using coloured paper. Use gold and silver paper if possible, but recycled wrapping paper or other coloured paper will also be fine. Using the glue, stick the paper squares onto the fish shape to create scales. With some ingenuity children will discover ways of overlapping the scales and getting them into patterns (stripes, blobs *etc*.). To finish, draw an eye with a black marker pen. If making a large classroom display, each child can make their own small fish, and work as a class to decorate one huge fish – the magical fish from our story. Stage the display with groups of small fish surrounding the magical fish.